the story of

NOAH

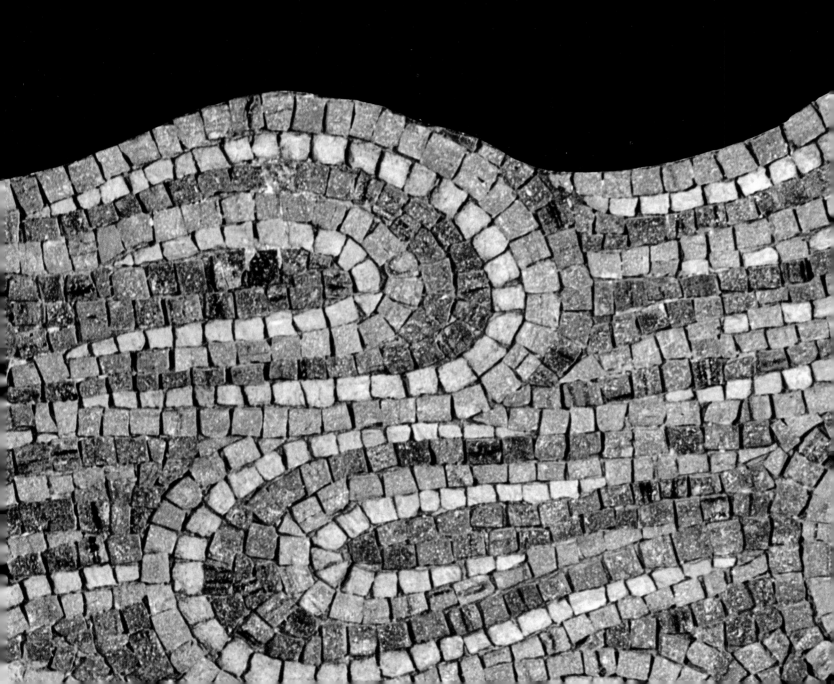

AND IT CAME TO PASS,

when men began to multiply
on the face of the earth,
and daughters were born unto them,
That the sons of God saw the daughters
of men that they were fair; and they took
them wives of all which they chose.
And the LORD said, My spirit shall not
always strive with man,
for that he also is flesh: yet his days
shall be an hundred and twenty years.

There were giants in the

and also after that, when the sons of God
came in unto the daughters
of men, and they bare children to them, the same
became mighty
men which were of old, men of renown.

earth in those days;

And GOD saw that the wickedness of man
was great in the earth,
and that every imagination of the thoughts
of his heart was only evil continually.

And it repented the LORD that he had made man
on the earth, and it grieved him at his heart.

And the LORD said, I will destroy man whom I
have created from the face of the earth; both
man, and beast, and the creeping thing, and
the fowls of the air; for it repenteth me that
I have made them.

But Noah found grace
in the eyes of the LORD.

These are the generations of Noah:
NOAH was a just man
and perfect in his generations,

and Noah walked with God.

and Noah begat three sons, Shem, Ham, and Japheth.

*The earth also was corrupt before God, and the earth
was filled with violence.
And God looked upon the earth, and, behold, it was corrupt;
for all flesh had corrupted his way upon the earth.
And God said unto Noah, The end of all flesh is come before me;
for the earth is filled with violence through them;
and, behold, I will destroy them with the earth.*

MAKE THEE AN ARK

of gopher wood; rooms shalt thou make in the ark, and shalt pitch it within and without with pitch.

*And this is the fashion which
thou shalt make it of: The length of the ark
shall be three hundred cubits,
the breadth of it fifty cubits, and the height
of it thirty cubits.*

*A window shalt thou make to the ark, and in
a cubit shalt thou finish it above;
and the door of the ark
shalt thou set in the side thereof; with lower,
second, and third stories shalt thou make it.*

And, behold, I, even I, do bring a flood of waters upon the earth,
to destroy all flesh, wherein is the breath of life, from under heaven;
and every thing that is in the earth shall die.

But with thee will I establish my covenant

and thou shalt come into the ark, thou, and thy sons
and thy wife, and thy sons' wives with thee.

AND OF EVERY LIVING THING
of all flesh, two of every sort
shalt thou bring unto the ark, to keep them alive
with thee; they shall be male and female.

Of fowls after their kind,
and of cattle after their kind, of every creeping
thing of the earth after his kind, two of
every sort shall come unto thee to keep them alive.

And take thou unto thee
of all food that is eaten, and thou
shalt gather it to thee;
and it shall be for food for thee, and for them.

THUS DID NOAH
according to all that God commanded him,
so did he.

And the LORD said unto Noah

Come thou and all thy house into the ark:
for thee have I seen righteous before me
in this generation.

Of every clean beast
thou shalt take to thee by sevens,
the male and his female:
and of beasts that are not clean by two,
the male and his female.

Of fowls also of the air by sevens,
the male and the female; to keep seed alive
upon the face of all the earth.

For yet seven days, and I will cause it
to rain upon the earth forty days
and forty nights;
and every living substance
that I have made will I destroy
from off the face of the earth.

And Noah did according unto all that
the LORD commanded him.

And Noah was six hundred years old
when the flood of waters was upon the earth.

And Noah went in, and his sons, and his wife, and his sons' wives with him,
into the ark, because of the waters of the flood.
Of clean beasts, and of beasts that are not clean
and of fowls, and of everything that creepeth upon the earth.

There went in two and two
unto Noah into the ark,

the male and the female, as God had commanded Noah.

And it came to pass after seven days, that the waters of the flood were upon the earth.
In the six hundredth year of Noah's life, in the second month,
the seventeenth day of the month, the same day were all the fountains
of the great deep broken up,

And the windows of heaven were opened

And the rain was upon the earth forty days and forty nights.

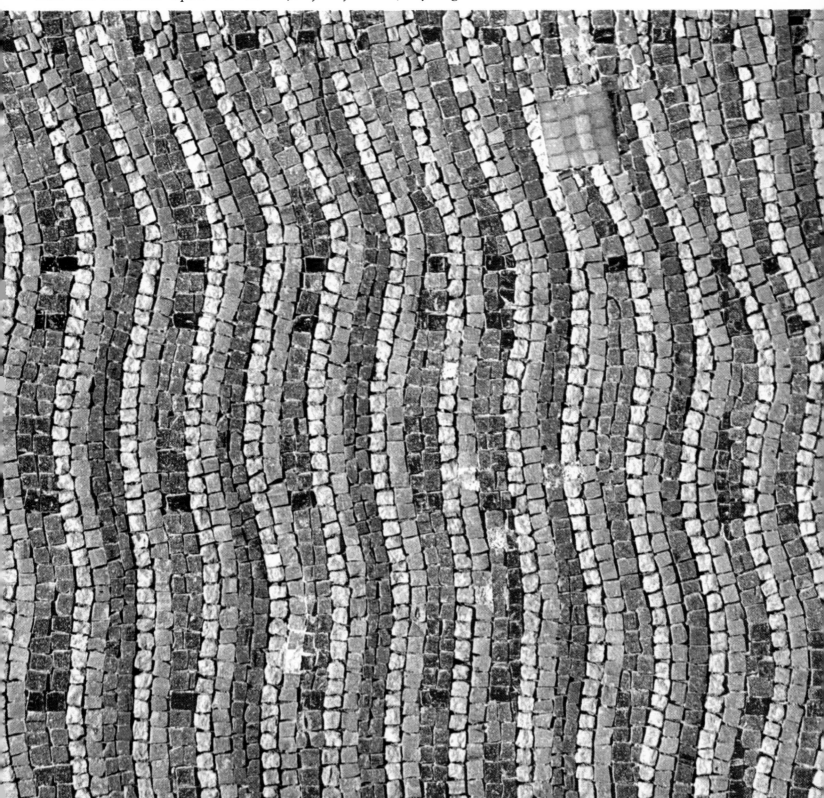

In the selfsame day entered Noah

and Shem, and Ham, and Japheth, the sons of Noah, and Noah's wife,
and the three wives of his sons with them, into the ark.
They, and every beast after his kind, and all the cattle after their kind,
and every creeping thing that creepeth upon the earth after his kind,
and every fowl after his kind, every bird of every sort.

And they went in unto Noah into the ark,

two and two of all flesh, wherein is the breath of life.
And they that went in, went in male and female of all flesh,
as God had commanded him: and the LORD shut him in.

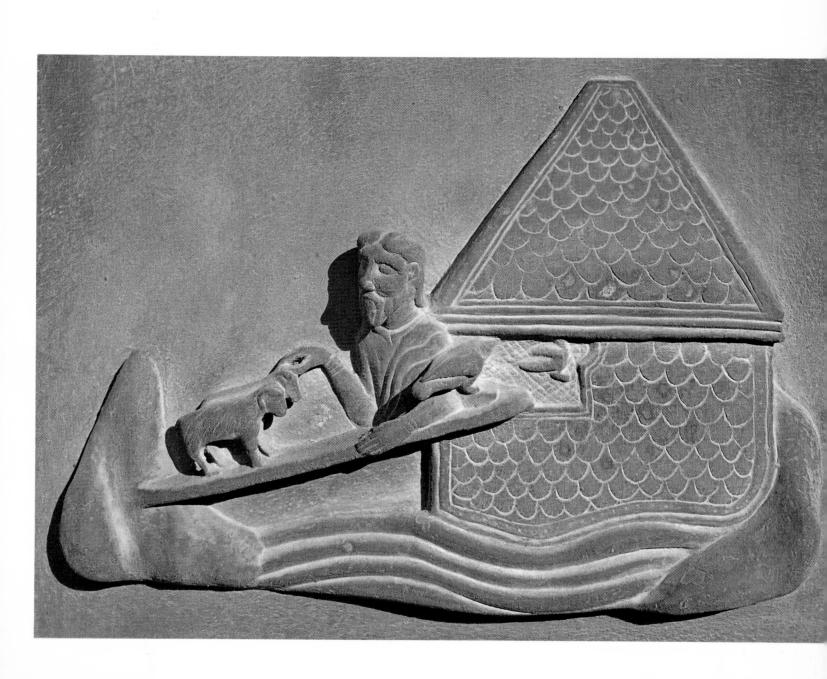

And the flood was forty days upon the earth

And the waters increased,
and bare up the ark,

And it was lift up above the earth.
And the waters prevailed, and were increased greatly upon the earth;
and the ark went upon the face of the waters.
And the waters prevailed exceedingly upon the earth;
and all the high hills that were under the whole heaven were covered.
Fifteen cubits upward did the waters prevail;
and the mountains were covered.

And all flesh died
that moved upon the earth,

*both of fowl, and of cattle and of beast, and of every creeping thing
that creepeth upon the earth, and every man.*

All in whose nostrils was the breath of life, of all that was in the dry land died.

And every living substance was destroyed which was upon the face of the ground, both man, and cattle, and the creeping things, and the fowl of the heaven; and they were destroyed from the earth: and Noah only remained alive, and they that were with him in the ark.

And the waters prevailed

upon the earth an hundred and fifty days.

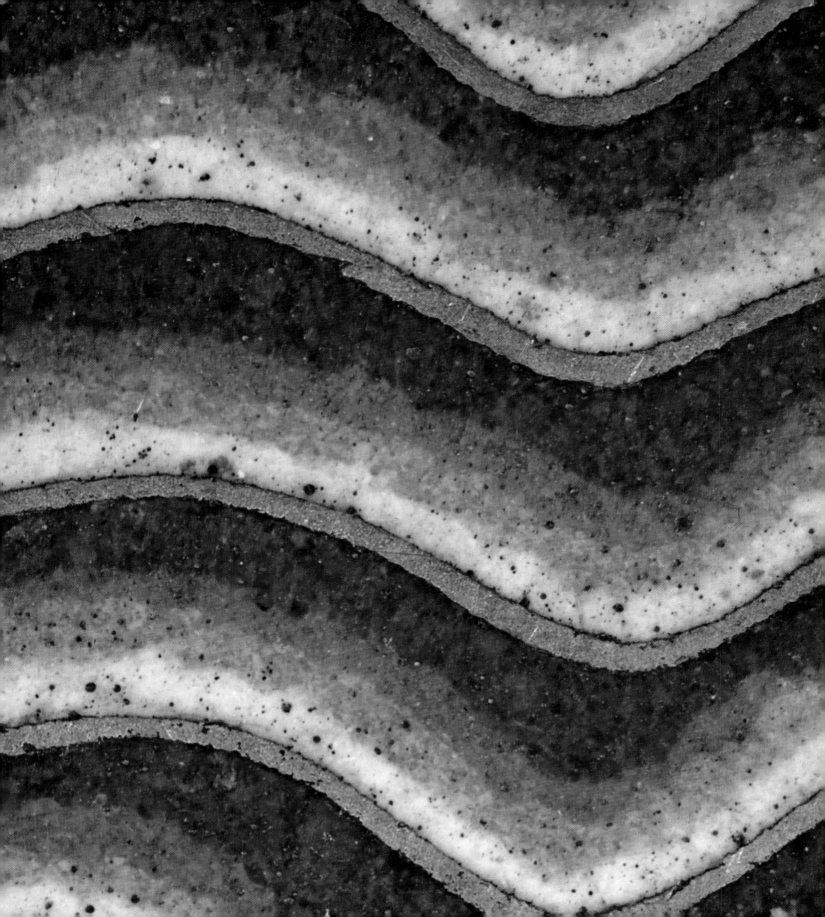

And God remembered Noah, and every living thing,

and all the cattle that was with him in the ark:
and God made a wind to pass over the earth, and the waters assuaged.
The fountains also of the deep and the windows of heaven were stopped,
and the rain from heaven was restrained.
And the waters returned from off the earth continually:
and after the end of the hundred and fifty
days the waters were abated.

And the ark rested

in the seventh month, on the seventeenth day of the month, upon the mountains of Ararat.

And the waters decreased

continually until the tenth month: in the tenth month,
on the first day of the month, were the tops of the mountains seen.

And it came
to pass
at the end
of forty days,
that Noah
opened
the window
of the ark
which he
had made:

And he sent forth a raven

which went forth to and fro,
until the waters were dried up from off the earth.

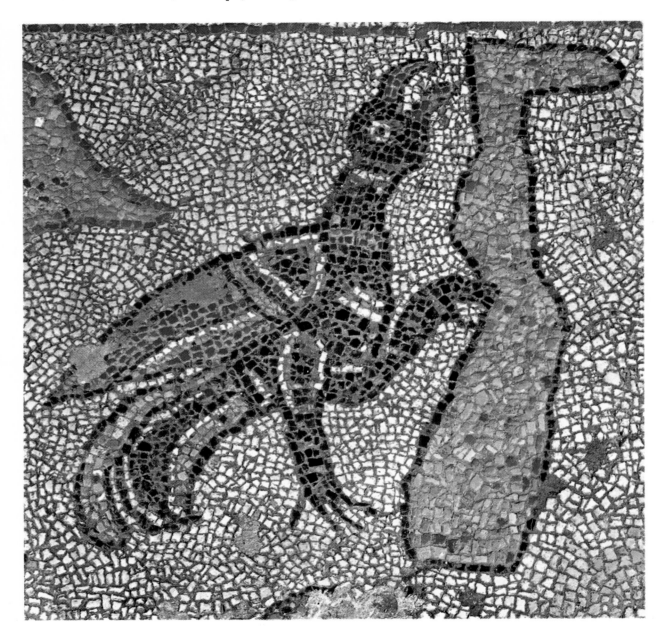

Also he sent forth a dove

from him, to see if the waters were abated from off the face of the ground;
But the dove found no rest for the sole of her foot, and she returned unto him into the ark,
for the waters were on the face of the whole earth:
then he put forth his hand, and took her,
and pulled her in unto him into the ark. And he stayed yet another seven days; and again he sent
forth the dove out of the ark; And the dove came to him in the evening;

And, lo, in her mouth was an olive leaf plucked off:

So Noah knew that the waters were abated
from the earth.
And he stayed yet other seven days;

And he stayed yet another seven days;
and again

And sent forth the dove;

which returned not again unto him
any more.

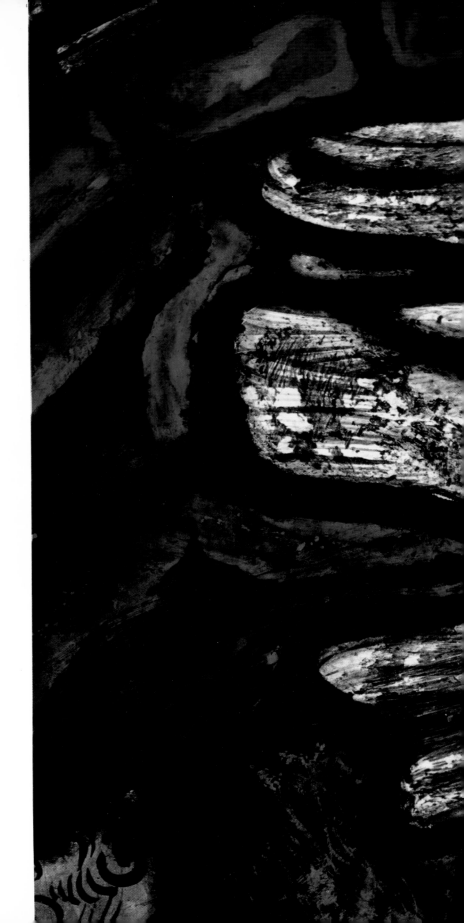

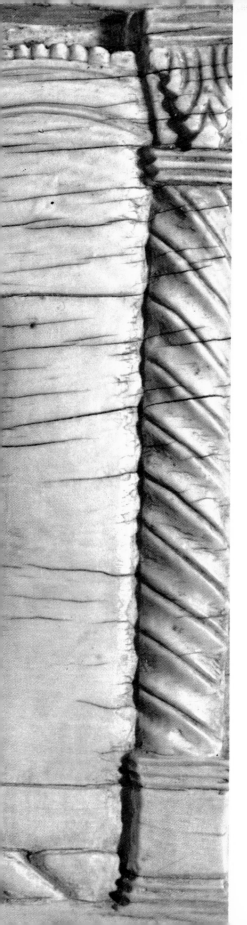

And it came to pass in the six hundredth and first year,
in the first month, the first day of the month,
the waters were dried up from off the earth:

and Noah removed the covering of the ark,

and looked, and, behold, the face of the ground was dry.

And in the second month,
on the seven and twentieth day of the month, was the earth dried.

And God spake unto Noah, saying

Go forth of the ark, thou, and thy wife,
and thy sons, and thy sons' wives with thee.

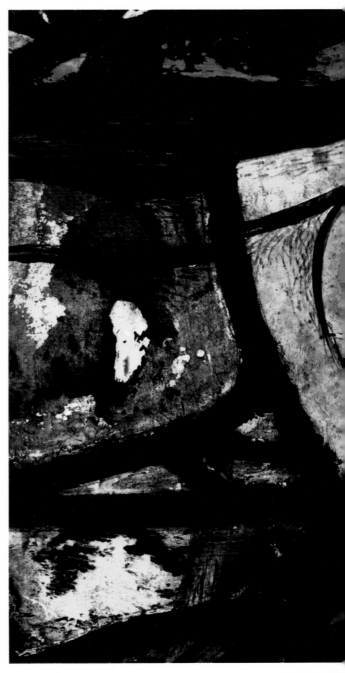

Bring forth with thee every living thing

that is with thee, of all flesh,
both of fowl, and of cattle, and of every creeping thing that creepeth upon the earth;
that they may breed abundantly in the earth, and be fruitful, and multiply upon the earth.
And Noah went forth, and his sons, and his wife, and his sons' wives with him:
Every beast, every creeping thing, and every fowl, and whatsoever creepeth upon the earth,
after their kinds, went forth out of the ark.

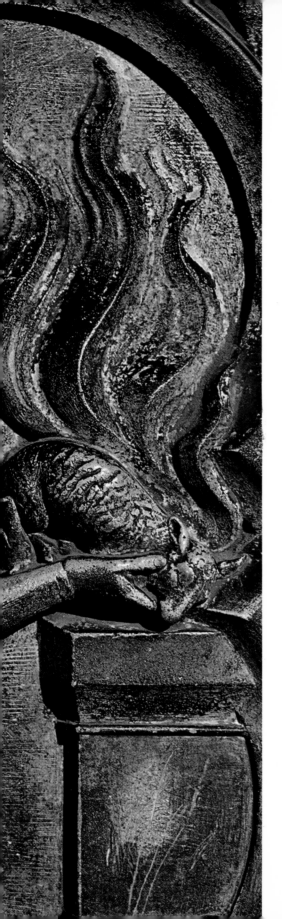

And Noah builded an altar unto the Lord;

and took of every clean beast, and of every clean fowl,
and offered burnt offerings on the altar.
And the LORD smelled a sweet savour;
and the LORD said in his heart,
I will not again curse the ground any more
for man's sake; for the imagination of man's heart
is evil from his youth; neither will I
again smite any more every thing living, as I have done.
While the earth remaineth, seedtime and harvest,
and cold and heat, and summer and winter,
and day and night shall not cease.

And God blessed Noah and his sons, and said unto them, Be fruitful, and multiply, and replenish the earth.

*And the fear of you and the dread of you
shall be upon every beast of the earth,
and upon every fowl of the air,
upon all that moveth upon the earth,
and upon all the fishes of the sea;
into your hand are they delivered.
Every moving thing that liveth shall be meat for you;
even as the green herb have I given you all things.
But flesh with the life thereof,
which is the blood thereof, shall ye not eat.
And surely your blood of your lives will I require;
at the hand of every beast will I require it,
and at the hand of man;
at the hand of every man's brother will I require
the life of man.
Whoso sheddeth man's blood, by man shall his blood
be shed: for in the image of God made he man.
And you, be ye fruitful, and multiply;
bring forth abundantly in the earth,
and multiply therein.
And God spake unto Noah,
and to his sons with him saying,
And I, behold, I establish my covenant with you,
and with your seed after you;
And with every living creature that is with you,
of the fowl, of the cattle, and of every beast
of the earth with you; from all that go out of the ark,
to every beast of the earth.
And I will establish my covenant with you;
neither shall all flesh be cut off any more by the waters
of a flood; neither shall there any more
be a flood to destroy the earth.*

And Noah awoke from his wine,
and knew what his younger son had done
unto him.
And he said,
Cursed be Canaan;
a servant of servants shall he be
unto his brethren.

And he said, Blessed be the LORD God of Shem;

and Canaan shall be his servant.

God shall enlarge Japheth, and he shall dwell
in the tents of Shem; and
Canaan shall be his servant.

And Noah lived after the
flood three hundred and fifty years.

And all the days of Noah
were nine hundred and fifty years: and he died.

*The brief but dramatic story
of Noah and his Ark is one of the best loved
of all Bible tales.*

Told and re-told long before it was first put into written form some 2,400 years ago, it has since given rise to epics, operas, learned tomes and picture books, even night-club monologues, rock-and-roll songs and children's toys. The Bible itself, both in the Old Testament and the New, makes repeated use of Noah's image as a righteous man and of the moral of his journey in the Ark.

But Noah's story is far more than an ancient Christian tale. Long before the birth of Christ it was an important part of Hebrew tradition. The main plot of the story—a flood which destroyed the world, and a man designated by a god who rode it out and then replanted the seeds of life—goes back at least 4,000 years. And there are traces of pagan religions that go even further back, to times when men worshipped the many gods and demons who, for them, ruled the elements. But most fascinating of all, perhaps, to Christians is the way in which theologians and Biblical commentators as long ago as medieval times, recognized in Noah a pre-figuration of Christ—an interpretation which links the very basis of the Christian religion to Judaism and the worship of cosmic gods.

Looking at the Noah story in its simplest form, the reasoning behind such an interpretation is not too difficult to see. It is the tale of a man chosen by God to save the world. God, having made man and all other living creatures, looks upon the results and decides to destroy it all, as a punishment to man for his violent and corrupt ways. However, He finds one man who is just and good, and this decides Him to try once more to create the perfect world He has envisaged. He orders Noah to build a huge Ark and fill it with a representative selection of all the animals on earth, and then He sends a Flood to destroy everything that lives. Noah and his passengers float safely through the deluge, and after forty days and forty nights, God causes the waters to abate. Noah thereupon scouts the land, first with a raven, then with a dove, and finding that the earth had indeed dried out, disembarks with all the animals and immediately sets about cultivating the new world.

Mosaics, St. Mark's Cathedral, Venice

Endpapers
Title page
pages 4-5

The power of the Republic of Venice
was so great in 1073 that its ruler, the Doge Domenico Contarini
decided to demolish the Cathedral of St. Mark
and build a temple that would better reflect the wealth of the city.
The result, a Byzantine basilica
in the form of a Greek cross of such magnificence
that it is called "the chest of gold",
a name inspired by the rich marble and mosaic decor.

page 32

The glowing and romantic
mosaics from which the illustrations
of this book are drawn cover
the walls of the atrium,
the arcaded area
leading to the nave.

pages 36-37

page 40

The work of 13th century Venetian
craftsmen, they recount
a unique cycle of Biblical stories
from the Creation to the Exodus.
(The hand on the opposite
page is also from St. Mark's.)

Mosaics, St. Mark's Cathedral, Venice

page 49

*cover
pages 62-63*

pages 72-73

pages 76-77

Contrary to what most people think, this theme of an evil world destroyed by a flood but recreated through the virtue of one man is by no means unique to the Bible. It has its counterpart in an astonishing number of mythological traditions. One collector of Flood myths compiled no less than 88 different versions of the story from Asia, Africa, Europe, Australia, the South Sea Islands and both North and South America. Noah is Yima in Persia, Ut-napishtim in Babylonia, Deucalion in Greece, Manu in India and Montezuma to the Papago Indians of Arizona.

This is extraordinary testimony to the universality of the Noah story, but even more important, it shows how people in all ages have sought, consciously or unconsciously, for guidelines to the mysteries of existence. Stories and myths such as those of the Creation and Noah help to explain the origin and the renovation of the world. The similarities between the various versions, widely different though their origin may be, indicate that there are certain emotional needs basic to all mankind. In the case of Noah and the other Flood myths, it is a yearning for a Paradise that existed in the beginning of time but was destroyed through the wantonness of man. That such a yearning still exists today, even in the matter-of-fact mind of modern western man, is amply demonstrated by psychology.

There is one way, however, in which the story of Noah differs from the rest of Flood mythology: it ends with God making a pact with mankind, a covenant in which he promises never again to destroy the world in punishment for man's sins.

At the same time, God pledges to respect the cosmic and earthly forces of the natural elements. This is a complete break with the old beliefs of pagan nature religions that the skies and the waters, the forests and the fields were ruled by a variety of deities and demons who dominated the order of day and night and the cycle of the seasons. The people of the Middle Ages had themselves only recently forsaken these beliefs, and thus the Genesis account of God's covenant with Noah had a special and powerful appeal for them. It affirmed that the natural order of things was determined by a single

Supreme Being who had manifested a personal concern for the welfare of mankind.

Thus Christianity had a very personal appeal for the people of the Middle Ages, and its flowering was the salient feature of the medieval era. After the conversion of the Emperor Constantine in the 4th century, it was elevated to the status of a State religion, and the last of the pagan temples, which had been devoted to the worship of the secular ruler or the many gods of nature, were closed down. Gradually the Fathers of the Church constructed an intellectual edifice housing a concept of the universe formed according to Christian beliefs; and within it, to an everincreasing degree, the searching, fear-filled minds of medieval men and women found sanctuary and comfort.

Hand in hand with this intellectual evolution there came a great flowering of Christian art. For a people who could not read or write, the only means of mass communication was pictures, and the Church made full use of them. Paintings, sculptures, stained-glass windows and the great churches, cathedrals and monasteries to house them rose all over Europe. These were works created for the age, and today they still reflect the quality of the medieval mind. Majestic, calm and beautiful, they are the products of a devout, superstitious yet literal people: the stories and the symbols they depict were very real to medieval man, and are shown as such.

THE MANY VERSIONS OF NOAH

The citizen of the Middle Ages understood the Noah story on several levels. First, it was to him the literal account of a tremendous and catastrophic event in history. Then, it was the moral tale of a good man who had reaped his just reward. Finally, it was a mystical tale revealing the omnipotence of God.

It is this latter view that is most revealing of the mentality of medieval man, who saw the world and everything that happened in it as an expression of God's will. In this view, the spiritual world was every bit as real as the physical one; and a

Window, Chartres Cathedral

pages 6-7

Ever since the Druids celebrated religious rites around a well located here, the site of the Cathedral of Chartres in France has been a vital center of worship.
Thus, after fire destroyed most of the edifice in 1194, kings and princes, barons and citizens, peasants and workers flocked to contribute time and money for its reconstruction.

page 13

Among the gifts was a 42-pane stained glass window depicting the entire story of Noah.
The first five panes showing medieval coopers and cartwrights at work acknowledge the generosity of its donors, the members of those trade guilds.
Created between 1235 and 1240 in the workshops of Notre Dame of Paris, this window can still be seen immediately to the left of the entrance to the nave.

page 20

Window, Chartres Cathedral

pages 22-23

page 29

page 33

page 39

great many of the objects and manifestations of the physical world had spiritual meanings. A rainbow was a rainbow, a dazzling display of color in the heavens; but it was also a manifestation of the voice of God. A flood was a physical disaster; but it was also an expression of God's displeasure, and hence to be suffered stoically as a punishment. Birds, fishes and other animals; trees, flowers and herbs shared these double meanings—and the key to this world of two—fold meanings wa's the Bible.

The principal characters of the story also assumed a double meaning, or double identity. In the early Middle Ages, the belief was strong that labor was a penitence. After the 12th century, it became a Christian virtue, a form of insurance that would pay off on the Day of Judgement, when the good and bad acts of men and women were totted up to determine their salvation or damnation. Noah was a hardworking man who carried out unquestioningly the command of God. As the builder of the Ark, therefore, he was adopted as a model and a patron saint by both the shipwrights and the carpenters of medieval times. As the first man to make wine (and the first to be intoxicated by it) he also became the patron saint of the coopers. To the serfs, he was a symbol of the pact they had with their masters—the heart of the feudal system—for Noah had made a covenant with God: hence it was natural to portray him, as in the mosaic on page 25, dressed in the clothing of a vassal as he received God's word.

Noah's three sons, too, who are pictured on page 13 in a stained-glass window of the cathedral of Chartres, were important symbols of the social hierarchy in medieval times. Feudal society was rigidly divided into three classes: those who prayed, those who fought, and those who worked. The destinies of Shem, Japhet and Ham (also called Canaan) in Genesis were taken as justification of this: the first two were believed to have engendered the clergy and the chivalric knights, while Ham, cursed by Noah for having spied upon his nakedness (pp. 92-93) was believed to have been the originator of the serfs and the working class.

Even the notion that God could actually destroy the world if He so chose fitted neatly into the medieval mind, conditioned as it was by its history of bloody infidel invasion, recurrent and devastating famines, and periodic epidemics of dread and little understood disease. Life was a perilous proposition at best in those times, with a descent into Hell on the Day of Judgement looming as a certain fate for sinners. The notion that a cruel and wicked world had once already been destroyed, with Noah starting a new and better one, seemed entirely possible and at times even desirable.

But the overriding interpretation of Noah was a strongly mystical one. Noah was chosen by God to save the world, and in medieval theology as well as in the deeply pious popular mind, this meant that he prefigured Jesus Christ, the Saviour. And this in turn led to the belief that the voyage of Noah's Ark on the purifying waters of the Flood was nothing less than the symbol of the baptismal rite, the washing with the sanctified water which inaugurates the life of every Christian. And to the people of the Middle Ages, this was the most meaningful of all their religious ceremonies.

Most of our knowledge of these deeper meanings which manifest themselves in medieval art and thinking come from the works of theological scholars who built the intellectual foundation of the Church. This building was not an easy task; the pagan religions died hard, and even among early Christians there were those who challenged, for example, the orthodox views on the nature of Jesus Christ. Under this pressure, the Church was forced to declare that not only were the events in the Old and New Testaments historical truths and evidence that there truly existed only one God, the Father of all mankind, but that the advent of Christ was the fulfillment of a Divine plan for the salvation of the world. To buttress these far-ranging arguments, a growing body of believers whom we know today as "Apologists" went to considerable lengths in researching and presenting documentation.

One method was to point out analogies between the Old Testament (the accepted historical record of what happened before Christ) and the New Testament (the compilation of Christian beliefs). Known as typology, this furnished an historical

page 48

pages 68-69

page 74

Window, Chartres Cathedral

page 74

pages 74-75

pages 82-83

bridge between the events known to have happened before Christ and those foretold by Christian teachings. The repetition of events in the Bible seemed to form a pattern of Divine behavior, and the faithful, both clergy and lay, felt they had gained some insight into the Divine plan for man's salvation.

Thus typology (and elementary psychology) shaped the intellectual foundations of the medieval world; to the artists and artisans who built the great churches and filled them with works of art fell the task of transmitting these teachings to the common man. If we are struck today by the power and majesty of their creation, it is even more impressive to realize the carefully thought-out meanings which they convey. For they were constructed in accordance with a precise and strictly followed set of rules—a kind of graphic theological code which gave each work an important intellectual as well as artistic function. For example, while the Old Testament stories were always faithful to their Hebrew authors, they also contained the symbols which formed the code to the spiritual elements of Christianity. An aureole surrounding the body, in this subtle but universally understood language, expressed eternal bliss. God the Father, Jesus Christ, the angels and the apostles were always shown with bare feet; the Virgin and the saints, however, were not. The Virgin was always shown with a veil, symbol of her virginity; Jews, after 1215, were always identified by the cone-shaped caps they wore, and any city with an angel on its battlements was Jerusalem.

In this way, the stories in paintings and stone could be read by medieval men who knew the language of symbols; and as one "reads" the story of Noah today through the eyes, as it were, of the artists who created it, the universality of its theme becomes ever more apparent. It is a story that begins with water—the formless void from which, as the Genesis relates it, God created dry earth, fruitful plants, living animals and, finally, man. To medieval man, this formless void was just as real as the H-bomb is to us today: it was at the very beginning of things, at the limit of his imagination of how he came to be; and it was also at the end of things, the nothingness to which God could at any time return him and the world, as indeed He did in Noah's time. The mosaic of water shown at the beginning of this book, therefore, was something which a medieval viewer would regard with awe as the symbol of the fate which, once before, had befallen wicked man.

What was the state of the world in Noah's time, as shown in these pictures? There were "giants on the earth" (pp. 6, 7). Men in the beginning of time were larger, more powerful and longer-lived than the people of the Middle Ages—Noah himself, at 500 years of age, was said to have produced three sons, and no medieval Christian would have questioned this figure. Indeed, Noah was a stripling compared to the first Babylonian kings which, according to tradition, had reigned for as long as 2,700 years each in the days before a flood had destroyed their world. After this catastrophe, they went into a decline, with their reigns becoming progressively shorter—a mythological tradition which fitted perfectly into the medieval view that civilization was going downhill: "The men of the past were handsome and strong", complained one writer of the 13th century. "Now they are children and dwarfs."

The giants on the earth, then, were symbols of a better time, of a power structure in what was a wealthy and rather civilized pre-Flood world. But in this world material things had assumed more importance than pious service to God. The ends had come to justify the means, and God at last saw that "wickedness was great upon the earth", and said: "I will destroy man whom I have created." To the devout men of medieval times, this pronouncement was entirely understandable: they spent most of their lives dodging the penalties for wickedness exacted by their feudal masters as well as the ever-present threat of the Devil and Hell painted by their clergy. Destruction in one form or another was a part of their daily lives.

In the corrupt civilization of pre-Flood times, however, one man—Noah—found grace, for he walked with God. The fact that this communion between the Lord and one of His subjects is shown literally, in the panel of carved ivory on pages 10 and 11, is an important indication of how medieval

page 87

page 89

pages 92-93

Altar, Cathedral of San Matteo, Salerno

pages 10-11

page 16

The museum of the cathedral in Italy today houses this former ivory altar piece of the cathedral, the work of local artisans who carved in relief 54 scenes from the Old and New Testament. Probably the largest work of this kind, for its day, it was made in the 9th century.

page 70

thinking was changing around the 11th century, when this panel was made. Until then, God the Father had been pictured only as a hand emanating from the heavens (p. 10 *et al*), a custom going straight back to the commandment God gave Moses that man could not see God and live. The Hebrew priests and their early Christian counterparts feared that their flocks might fall into idolatrous ways were they to depict God in the form of man. The fact that God could now be depicted full form, with only His hand, upraised in the divine blessing, and the halo around His head to indicate that He is indeed the Supreme Being, testified to the security which the new faith now enjoyed.

As for Noah, he received the manifestation of God's grace with due humility but not, as might perhaps be expected, with his head bowed in an attitude of prayer. His attitude as shown on page 9 is typical of medieval man: his eyes are turned toward Heaven, for it is from there that the word of God will come. And whatever it may be, he will accept it as his destiny, believing implicity in the implacable nature of God's command that he should build an Ark of gopher wood. He does not ask why, he does not ask how—it is sufficient that he has been commanded, and so he sets to work.

The task of building the Ark—commissioned by God with detailed measurements and specifications—is shown in fascinating detail in a variety of sculptures, bas-reliefs and stained-glass windows on pages 16 through 23. Here are clearly to be seen the tools and methods employed by medieval shipbuilders—particularly those of Italy, which at this time was just beginning to reconstruct its maritime fleets. Saws, hammers, adzes, planes and drills are used by the workmen, and as the works of art advance in time from the early Middle Ages (pp. 16) to the late 14th century (pp. 18 and 19), tools and methods grow even more sophisticated.

But the construction of the Ark represents more than a literal depiction of Noah's labors; it also symbolizes the building of the spiritual church. The finished Ark, as depicted in the magnificent window from the Cathedral of Chartres shown on pages 22-23, is as much a church as it is a ship, built to save mankind.

For the Apologists, those early scholars who bolstered the faith with analogies drawn between the Old and New Testaments, the finished Ark was a rich source of material. Some of their conclusions seem pushed to absurdity—St. Augustine, for example, figured out that Noah's Ark represented the Cross on which Christ died because the length of a man's body is six times as great as its width: the exact proportions of both the Ark and the Cross. But the principal theme has the kind of poetic logic which is at the heart of mythology and religion. In this view, Noah's voyage on water which saved life on earth is clearly seen as a prefiguration of Christ's death to save mankind.

The reasoning behind this interpretation is complex but interesting. Water is at the heart of it—water as a symbol of the formlessness from which the world was created, and also as the prime source of life (both views, incidentally, which modern science has now confirmed by physical and chemical, rather than religious research). In the Noah story, water was used as a means of destroying life—i.e. returning the world to formlessness—and the instrument of man's salvation was an Ark, made of wood. But the water which destroyed the world also purified it—a powerful argument for the efficacy of the baptismal rite, in which the body is plunged into water and re-emerges, cleansed of its original sin and endowed with the new, pure life of the Church. Thus the Noah story symbolizes death, rebirth, purification and salvation—just as does the story of Christ, who descended into the formlessness of death for man's sake, then re-emerged to take His place at the right hand of God. And here the instrument of man's salvation was, like the Ark, another wooden object: the Cross.

Noah and his sons labored on the Ark in total ignorance of what it was to be used for: they had only God's word that they should build it. There were no signs of approaching disaster, and it may be justifiably assumed that Noah's stubborn insistence on building his monstrosity made him the butt of gibes by contemporaries bent on finding easier ways to harvest their earthly reward. But when the Ark was finally completed Noah got his full reward (pp. 24, 25): God made a covenant

Altar, Klosterneuburg

page 9

The magnificent altar from which this detail was taken stands today in the Austrian monastery of Klosterneuburg, near Vienna. Its three panels contain 51 enamelled plaques depicting God's plan for the salvation of mankind. This triptych is one of only two known works of a 12th century master of the enameller's art known as Nicholas of Verdun; thus the work is known as the Verdun altar. Originally conceived as panelling for a chancel, it was transformed into an altar panel in 1331, after a disastrous fire virtually destroyed the monastery (Nicholas' great work was saved by pouring wine over it).

pages 52-53

page 54

page 65

Millstatt Manuscript, Carinthian Provincial Museum, Klagenfurt

page 15

pages 80-81

*These red, blue and brown ink drawings were
penned in the 11th or 12th centuries by a Benedictine
monk of the Millstatt Monastery
in Carinthia Austria.
The drawings, 87 in all,
illustrate poems on the Genesis and
Exodus chapters of the Old Testament.*

Capital; Sainte Madelaine Basilica, Vezelay

*In 1120, more than a thousand pilgrims had gathered
in this church to pray
at a tomb containing relics of Mary Magdelane
when a catastrophic fire swept through and destroyed the nave.
Reconstruction began immediately.
By 1140, the stone capitals in the nave had all been carved
out of local stone with the lyrical realism for which
the artisans from this devout region in Burgundy were famous.
The sculpture depicting the construction of the Ark
is located in the upper part of the central nave on the south side.*

page 17

with him, His first, in which He promised that Noah alone, with his crew and his complement of animals, would survive the destruction He was about to wreak upon the world. So Noah set about the job of collecting his passengers and getting them aboard.

The medieval bestiary depicted in this book to show how Noah got his animals together is no doubt a combination of fact and fantasy, but it, too, is subject to the medieval artist's graphic code: each animal plays an important symbolic role in the story. The lion, for instance, is properly portrayed as the king of beasts on page 35, leading the rest of the animals. To the medieval viewer he is also a symbol of Christ's Resurrection. It was believed at the time that lion cubs, once born, showed no signs of life for three days, until the lion himself breathed upon and brought them alive—a legend recalling Christ's sojourn in the tomb. The pelican seen stalking toward the Ark on page 32 is likewise a Resurrection symbol: it was said that the mother pelican killed her young after they hatched, and then revived them by opening her breast and sprinkling them with blood. The snakes, of course, were symbols of evil, members of the group of unclean animals which God commanded Noah to take with him.

Among the human passengers, Noah's wife had a particular symbolic value. For one thing, she represented Eve, who brought about the fall of man. In another vein, she has gone down in legend as the eternal shrew, bickering and complaining as she is doing in the stained glass window from Chartres Cathedral shown on page 39. Still other versions, inspired by the apocryphal gospels popular at the time, have her in collusion with the Devil, who was anxious to learn why Noah had a private line of communication with God. These noncanonical scriptures were probably responsible for the generally low opinion of women prevailing in the Middle Ages.

When the passengers, animal and human, were all safely gathered in the Ark the rains came—a deluge of waters from the "windows of Heaven" which God had opened, as depicted in the strong vertical lines of the mosaic on pages 36-37. In the scenes of violence and agony and death which follow, the medieval artist was in his element, for here is all the wrath of the pagan nature gods of a still unforgotten past, let loose in a dramatic, swirling torrent that sweeps all life before it. For 40 days and 40 nights the rains fall, and the Ark is borne upon the stormy waters until at last all life has drowned and calm prevails (pp. 52, 53).

The anxiety felt by Noah and his passengers throughout the violence of the deluge was a familiar emotion to a people who lived in an age still deeply affected by a barbaric past, and it is depicted with telling impact on pages 54 and 55. But then, at long last, the Ark came to rest on the peak of Mount Ararat (p. 56), and Noah could gaze forth in wonderment at his salvation. The Genesis story has him opening a window in the Ark and looking out; in the 4th century, a very early Christian artist depicted this moving moment in a scene chiseled on a tomb in the catacombs of Rome (pp. 58, 59). Christianity was still a clandestine religion then, and the Noah shown is probably a symbol of the new religion as it struggled to establish itself openly in a hostile, pagan world. More personally, Noah is also seen as a soul that has been saved by the prayers said by early worshippers in the Office of the Dead.

Why is Ararat, which is in Armenia, named as the place where the Ark at last ran aground? It is a long way from there to the Biblical lands where Noah's voyage began, and scholars still do not agree why the Hebrew scribes chose this as Noah's ultimate destination. But the legend has persisted through the ages, fortified from time to time by reports, even in modern times, that traces of the Ark have actually been sighted there.

Geographical considerations apart, however, the Ark came to rest in a place that was entirely logical to a devout Christian mind: Ararat was the highest peak known to man in that part of the world, and as such it was the closest point on earth to God. Throughout the Christian era—and even before, in such religions as that of the Sumerians, originally a mountain people who built temples resembling mountains on the flat plains of Mesopotamia— mountain peaks have been a familiar symbol of

Enamel plaque, Saint-Pierre Cathedral treasury Troyes

page 86

Noah the Husbandman is depicted reaching up to pick the grapes from his vines. The plaque is thought to have been painted about 1160 by an anonymous French artisan of Troyes, possibly to decorate a home.

Choir Stalls, Cologne Cathedral

page 91

The marvelously carved choir stalls in the great cathedral of Cologne are—like the cathedral itself—the largest in all Germany. There are 104 stalls in all, carved in oak, abounding in figures of all kinds, human, animal and demonic, taken from all manner of myths, Biblical tales and themes of classical antiquity. The scene of Noah's drunkenness is probably a restoration; the stalls themselves date from the early 14th century.

Tomb, Santa Priscilla Catacombs, Rome

The touchingly primitive Noah etched on marble can be seen deep inside one of the most ancient of all Christian cemeteries, the catacombs of Rome. Founded before the middle of the second century by Priscilla, a noble Roman lady who was an early convert, these subterranean sepulchres housed the dead of her family, of the first Christian martyrs, and several popes as well as the poor Christians of Rome. The graves of the latter were cut out of the walls and closed with rough tiles or marble slabs carved with symbols and inscriptions like this one on a 4th century slab, which is photographed for the first time. The catacombs are located on the Via Salaria Nova less than a mile from the former Gate of Salaria.

pages 58-59

Capital, Gerona Cathedral Cloister

page 17

pages 42-43

*The massive figures carved on a stone capital
in this early 12th century cloister in Gerona, Spain,
were created in a period often called "the great age of stone".
The principle function of this romanesque art, so closely integrated
with the architecture of the church, was to make the church "speak".
The capitals of pilasters and columns were a favorite location
for anecdotal friezes depicting Biblical tales
in the familiar clothes and gestures of daily life—in this case those
of Catalonia in northeast Spain.*

Altar, Cathedral of Pistoia

pages 18-19

page 28

*One of the major works
of the silversmith's art in Italy,
the altar of the Chapel
of Saint James shows the story
of Noah and Flood
among other tales from the
Old Testament on its right side panel.*

communication with the deities, the most familiar of all, perhaps, being the church steeple.

Having looked out upon the world, Noah next sent a messenger forth to explore it: a raven. In Hebrew terms, the raven is an impure bird, an eater of carrion fit only to consort with the dead. But in medieval symbolism the raven is an ambiguous bird, sometimes good, sometimes evil. It is depicted, therefore, as pecking at the corpses still floating on the waters—in this sense, the raven fulfills its mission of verifying that God's will has been accomplished and that indeed no living thing remains on earth.

The dove, by contrast, was sent forth to see if the earth was fit for habitation once again. In modern times, the dove has come to serve political ideology: it is most commonly known as the symbol of peace. In medieval times, however, it had a different meaning—it represented the Holy Spirit, and as such it appears and reappears in depictions of the Trinity. Hugh of St. Victor, a Noah scholar and mystic philosopher of the 12th century, takes the typological view, describing the two ways of Christian life, the active and the contemplative. The blue feathers of its wings, in his view, are the Christian's thoughts of heaven; and it has red feet even as the Church, moving through the world, finds its feet stained with the blood of martyrs.

On its second trip, the dove returned, and "lo, in her mouth was an olive leaf pluckt off". This was interpreted not only as literal proof that the earth had dried and that plants were growing again, but also as the symbol of the new-found peace between god and man. The choice of this particular tree by the Hebrew authors of the Noah story was based less on any spiritual meaning attached to it than on the fact that the olive was and still is an essential part of life in Biblical lands, providing food and oil. In the medieval Christian church consecrated olive oil was used as a healing sacrament or for conferring the Holy Spirit during the baptismal ceremony.

After disembarking his passengers on dry land (once again the lion led the way: pp. 74, 75), Noah's first act was to build an altar upon which he made burnt offerings to the Lord (pp. 78-79).

In terms of the history of both Judaism and Christianity, this was a momentous event, for this was the first altar to be dedicated to the one and only God. The sacrificial offering, a practice dating from the worship of pagan nature gods, indicates the universality of the one God, who can be known and understood by all, pagans and believers, Christians and Jews.

The fire which Noah built upon his altar brought to the Lord a "sweet savor"—it is also the first mention of fire in the Book of Genesis.

Thus life began on earth again, and the Lord was pleased with what He had wrought and with the conduct of the man He chose to save. No longer would He curse the ground for man's sake; henceforth He would respect the natural order of the cosmos and leave unchanged the cycle of the seasons. Few words could have had greater import for the men of medieval times than those which God now spoke in His heart: "While the earth remaineth, seedtime and harvest, and cold and heat, and summer and winter, and day and night shall not cease." For not only did God thereby agree to leave unaltered the universal cycles of the world; by implication He also removed for all time the power of any other divinity to change them. Thus the pagan nature gods who vied with the one god for the adherence of the Hebrews were at last dethroned. While man's own destiny might still be shaky and obscure, at least that of the world he lived in was now fixed forever.

In recognition of this, after blessing Noah and his sons, God made a pact with them and for all future generations: "Neither shall all flesh be cut off any more by the waters of a Flood; neither shall there be any more Flood to destroy the earth..." And in a dramatic and moving gesture God concluded: "I do set my bow in the cloud and it shall be for a token of the covenant between me and the earth."—and there appeared a rainbow (pp. 84-85). For Hebrew and Christian alike, the image of the rainbow was now a token of the direct line of communication between the one and only God and His people. Indeed, it sealed the pact.

Thus ends the first part of the Noah story. The second cycle of events in his 950 years of life

page 21

page 64

The figures carved so gracefully out of stone on the upper porch of this gothic church represent 26 scenes from the Old Testament. Each scene is set within a square frame of four stylized leaves, a design widely used in the second half of the thirteenth century when the Crusader king, Saint Louis commissioned this chapel. He had just purchased the Sacred Crown of Thorns from Baudouin, Emperor of Constantinople, and needed a place to house it plus other sacred objects.

pages 78-79

Pierre de Montreuil, the leading French architect of the day, designed it, employing the most talented artisans of the city for the work. Among them were perhaps foreigners for Noah's Ark is designed

Portals, Sainte Chapelle, Paris

page 94

*like a 7th century Armenian church,
and he caulks
his Ark with pitch,
at technique used in the Middle East.
But the figures appearing
in the last three illustrations
of this book reflect
the humanism and love of life which
the artisans of that period were
able to express tenderly in stone.*

page 95

page 96

*These scenes,
though not from the Noah series,
tell of a new beginning.
Adam hoes while Eve spools yarn.
Eve nurses her baby—a typically
medieval reflection of the Virgin Mary—
while Adam grinds mill.
In the end,
thanks is given to God for His
gift of new life.*

presented medieval Biblical scholars with some problems as they sought to present him to the faithful as a forerunner of Jesus Christ. Here Noah is not the chosen man who saves mankind from flood and storm; there is nothing apocalyptic in his situation. He appears, rather, as a peaceful husbandman, and in his story the students of mythology trace certain traditions explaining the origins of agriculture.

Noah and his sons begin to farm the land, and Noah plants a vineyard (p. 86). When the grape is harvested, pressed and fermented, he drinks of the wine and becomes drunken. Viewed in its literal context—which is how the literal-minded man of medieval times would view it—this is not too surprising: Noah had never before tasted wine and did not know of its intoxicating power. More important, therefore, to the medieval apologists was the fact that he had planted seeds, as Jesus was to plant the seeds of the True Faith, and that these seeds flourished even as Christianity, after suffering and struggle, flourished in the world.

In his intoxication, Noah lies naked in his tent, a prefiguration of Christ stripped of His garments and humiliated on the road to Golgotha (pp. 90-91). Here he is seen by his youngest son Ham, also known as Canaan. The older brothers, Shem and Japheth, show more respect for their father: they take a cloak and, backing into the tent so that they will not see his shame, cover him as he lies there. For this, they are blessed with riches, while Ham is condemned to serve them. Shem went on to give his name to the race of Semites. Japheth begat sons who begat the distant peoples of the world, the Gentiles or non-Jews. For the Jews, this story served to explain the distribution of people in the world—as well as the fact that the land of Canaan was subjugated by two other nations.

As for Noah, he lived for another 350 years and died at last at the age of 950, still high in God's favor and a symbol of salvation to mankind.

Thus we find in the seemingly simple story of Noah religious themes drawn from the beliefs of pagan peoples, of Hebrew tribes, and finally of Christianity, all interwoven as in some vast tapestry. The many threads in the design as we know it in the Genesis are thought to have been woven together in Jerusalem, around the year 450 B.C., by an anonymous scribe working under the supervision of Ezra, the governor of the sacred city. Some of the threads were spun by the priests of the Temple of Solomon, which exists today only in the fragment known as the Wailing Wall. It is they who talked of the covenants, and who provided the precise figures for the measurements of the Ark and the duration of the deluge. Other elements reflect the concerns of a nomadic people, the Hebrew tribes from the south, who were interested in the destiny of man. To them we owe, for instance, a second version of the Creation, in chapter 2 of the Genesis, in which God as a village potter, makes man out of the dust of the earth.

The original design of our tapestry, however, must be traced back to Mesopotamia. Here the Hebrews, a conquered people, found themselves in exile after their own kingdom had been conquered by Nebuchadnezzar the Great first in 598 B.C., then again in 586 B.C. when the whole population including the priests were carried off and the Temple of Jerusalem was destroyed. The Chaldean king resettled his captives in Babylon, the capital of his kingdom, and long a center of political power in Mesopotamia.

For the Hebrews, their exile was an introduction to a culture and a religion that were in turn a result of several millennia of hybridization. Thrust into this world of multiple gods and many idols, the captives, led by the priests of their destroyed Temple, sought for strength within themselves and began the slow process of building a body of sacred doctrines and stories that would sustain their community through the centuries to come.

But the conquerors had a well-established society including its own sacred literature, the *Enumalish*. Their faith, strongly cemented by time, was a

page 25

The magnificent pavement of mosaics in the Cathedral of Maria Annunziata in Otranto, Italy, are the work of a humble, 12th century priest called Pantaleone. Crude but vigorous, they represent a Tree of Life that extends the whole length of the nave, its branches forming circles enclosing scenes from the Bible. It took Pantaleone from 1163 to 1166 to piece together his mosaic in this 11th century cathedral. Elsewhere, the art of mosaics was declining as a result of the schism between the East and West churches, but this region deep in Italy's heel had been conquered in 1059 by the Normans who promoted a synthesis of Byzantine mosaics with the monumental style of architecture favored in Rome.

page 60

Endpapers

114

Illuminated Manuscript, Histoire universelle en français de la création du monde jusqu'à César, Dijon

pages 34-35

pages 44-45

page 55

The 13th century was the century of encyclopedias when scholars attempted to organize all knowledge past and present. The anonymous cleric from Lille, France, who composed this manuscript about 1210 did not hesitate to embrace the history of the world from its creation by God through the Flood to the time of Caesar. He was commissioned to do so by Roger, the Governor of Lille. However, it is thought that the illuminations used in this book were created between 1260 and 1270 in Saint-Jean-d'Acre, then the residence of the Knights of Saint John and a part of the Kingdom of Jerusalem set up by the Crusaders. The manuscripts is number 562 in the library of Dijon, France.

Illuminated Manuscript, Beatus in Apocalipsin, Cathedral of Gerona

The painters of this manuscript used the vision of a world drowning while the Ark of Noah survives to illustrate a commentary on the Revelation of St. John the Divine. This apocalyptic vision of Christ's final victory over Satan and His second coming on the Day of Judgement held a place of honor in the Easter week liturgy of the Spanish Christians living under Moslem domination. Written originally about 784 by Beatus, the Abbot of the Monastery of San Martin de Liebano, and named after its author, the popular commentary was copied

pages 26-27

veritable mosaic of the many religions that had been assimilated by the peoples of this region during almost 500 years before the Hebrews came under their influence.

Four thousand years ago, this region was not the arid desert we know today, but a verdant crescent irrigated by the Tigris and Euphrates Rivers. It curved from the city of Ur, at the top of the Persian Gulf, northeastward into Turkey and southwestward down the coast of the Mediterranean Sea. This hospitable plain, strategically located between east and west, welcomed and sheltered successive waves of cultures. Peoples from the wild mountains of Beluchistan and the arid plateaus of Iran, roaming in search of a home, found there the fertile earth and mild climate conducive to the founding of prosperous civilizations.

The earliest civilization of which we have extensive knowledge is that of the Sumerians who surged out of the mountains to the east before 5,000 B.C. They built a series of cities, the most important of which was Ur. The Sumerians were followed by Semitic invaders, the Akkadians, who under Sargon I made their capital at Babylon. A third wave brought in the people who made Asshur on the upper Tigris their center of government, and were, consequently, known as Assyrians. Babylon, in the meantime, had been invaded by the Hittites, the Kassites and the Mittani, and finally, about 1,100 B.C. by the Assyrians.

The first Babylonian Empire, whose Sargon II was responsible for the deportation of the twelve Tribes of Israel from the northern Hebrew Kingdom, lasted until a confederation of the Semitic Chaldeans, the Medes and the Persians brought about its downfall in about 606 B.C. By the time the Hebrews came to Babylon, some 4,000 deities and daemons reigned over the skies, plains and cities of Mesopotamia. Yet also present was the Mittanic worship of a single high divinity represented by a solar disk. An ample store of myths and legends told of the origins of these gods and of the people who worshipped them. Many were already written down on the thin clay tablets used at this time and it is from the discovery of these tablets in the library at Ninevah built by the Assyrian king Assurbanipal that we know the Babylonian version of the creation of the world, and of the catastrophic deluge that followed.

The similarities between these myths and that of the Genesis are so marked that one irreverent scholar has described the Biblical version as a monotheistic poem composed in a Babylonian slum by a Hebrew refugee. Many Biblical scholars have also deduced that the flood of the Genesis and that of the Ninevah version are one and the same. Indeed, archaeological discoveries brought to light so many versions of it that it seems to have been a story universally accepted in all the great empires of the ancient middle east. Tablets were found in Nippur, an ancient Sumerian city. The Chaldeans and the Hittites wrote it down in their script and the Egyptians in theirs. It is not surprising that the Hebrews, fresh from the dry lands of Palestine and shaken by the disasters that had destroyed their Temple and swept away their people, made the story their own, seeing in it evidence of the same judgement that God had passed upon them when they had disobeyed His commandments and fallen into violent and idolatrous ways.

The Babylonian flood story is part of what is now called the Gilgamesh Epic and is to be found in the 11th canto. The poem relates the exploits of a man named Gilgamesh, who, during his search for the secret of immortality, visits a kinsman, Ut-Napishtim, who tells of an event in his own life. He was at the time of this experience a faithful follower of the god Ea. When the other gods decided to destroy the earth because of the violence rampant upon it, Ea warned Ut-Napishtim, ordering him to destroy his house and build a boat, whose dimensions the god designated. Representatives of all animals were to be taken aboard. The flood lasted seven days and seven nights, and then Ut-Napishtim sent out a dove, a raven and a swallow from the ark to ascertain if the waters had abated. Safely disembarked on dry land, Ut-Napishtim made an offering which was favorably received. As a sign of their blessing, the gods bestowed on him the jewels of Ishtar, the great goddess of creation. Ut-Napishtim became Noah for the exiles in Babylon, and Noah he has remained for the

Illuminated Manuscript,
Beatus in Apocalipsin, Cathedral of Gerona

pages 50-51

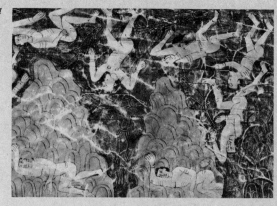

pages 30-31

several times over. This particular version was illustrated between 970 and 975 by the monk Emeterio.
A nun who signed herself "En Depintrix" had a helping hand in the illuminations. The manuscript is kept in the archives of the cathedral in Spain.

Illuminated Manuscript,
Vienna Genesis, Vienna National Library

pages 46-47

pages 84-85

Antakya, Turkey was a missionary center for early Christianity. Its theological school recruited its monks from the Syrian part of the population of whom eight painted the 48 miniatures late in the 6th century. Syrian monasteries had a monopoly on this parchment made from unborn calve's hide ranging from purple to pink. The ink now black was silver. The Crusaders probably carried it to Europe after taking the city from the Turks in 1098.

page 90

Door, Cathedral of Monreale

page 41

page 56

page 88

*Bonanno Pisano's bronze
bas-reliefs on the main door
of this cathedral near Palermo,
Sicily, mark a high point
in Italian medieval sculpture.
Dated 1186,
the figures on the 42 plaques
depicting Biblical scenes are remarkable
for their expressive simplicity.
The Cathedral was founded in 1174
by the Norman king, William II.*

millions who have read the Genesis.

Now, however we know much more about Ut-Napishtim and Noah than his authors could have ever imagined when they compiled the various elements of the Flood story in 450 B.C. Archaeological explorations have revealed what many scholars take to be the truth about the flood itself. In 1929, during explorations of the ancient site of Ur, capital of the Sumerian kingdom near the top of the Persian Gulf, excavations brought to light the royal sepulchres filled with a wealth of treasures in gold and silver, lapiz lazuli and bronze. After the workers had accomplished the tedious process of sifting through and removing these priceless items, they came to what they thought would be virgin soil—the bottom of the pit. But analysis of a sample of it revealed that it was clay, an alluvial soil that certainly could not be the solid mother earth generally found at the bottom of such diggings. The order was given to continue the excavations, and after shoveling through over three yards of the clay, the workers came upon yet another layer of relics. To the wonderment of all, this layer was from a totally different civilization and age. The brilliantly decorated pottery, for instance, was made on a potter's wheel, while those from the Sumerian people had been made by hand. The tools in this newest discovery dated from the Stone Age, while the Sumerians were of the Bronze Age. The nine-foot layer of alluvial soil thus represented a solid break in time between two civilizations.

Excavations were also made in other sites in Mesopotamia from Ur to Baluchistan, among them Susa, the Biblical Shushan of Esther; and Kish, located at a point where the Tigris and the Euphrates rivers flow close to each other. At each of these sites, archaeologists found a solid thick deposit of soil between the bottom layer and the one above it. In each case, the bottom layer contained the same decorated ceramics found at Ur, while the upper one was of another period. In each case, the society of men and women who had painted the pottery had somehow been cut off abruptly from any further activity. They had either suddenly abandoned the site, or suffered a catastrophy that simply wiped all life from the face of their world, leaving only these brilliantly colored fragments as proof of their existence. Logic told archaeologists that not even a period of drought or war could have caused such total abandonment. The only possibility was a flood of waters overflowing the banks of the rivers and surging out of the Persian Gulf, whipped into a fury by winds of cyclone force, such as Ut-Napishtim described as blowing "like an onslaught in battle as it rushed in on the people... The gods cowered like dogs, they crouched by the walls..."

Careful scrutiny of the traces left by these waters revealed that they had inundated an area estimated at 393 miles by 100 miles. The date: about 4,000 B.C.

Was this a local disaster or was it a time when floods descended upon people the world over? The fact that myths and legends about floods are to be found among nearly all the nations and tribes of the human race is frequently presented as an argument supporting the vision of a world-wide catastrophe.

However, whether the source is in the swirling mud-ladened waters of an inland river in spring or the cataclysmic force of a tidal wave, the destruction wrought leaves an indelible impression on the minds of men. In the face of such power, man can only tremble and wonder, for surely his acts unleashed this wrath. The Battaks of Sumatra say that the earth had grown old and ugly when Debata, the Creator, sent a flood to destroy every living thing. The ancient Greeks tell that fraud and cunning, violence and wicked lust had replaced virtue when Zeus burned with anger and sent a flood. In the time of the Roman Emperor Caesar Augustus, Ovid wrote that man first lived in the "golden age which of itself maintained the truth and right of everything..." But this ideal state of affairs did not last. In time, man became wicked and lawless. "Therein all mischief rushed forth... craft, treason, violence, envy, pride, and wicked lust to win." Jove therefore "fully determined the mortal kind to drown." But for all the remorsefulness, hope of better times springs eternally in man's heart. The waters will have washed away all the evil and permitted a righteous man to begin again.

Window, Wimpfen im Tal,
Monastery of St. Peter

page 57

pages 66-67

page 67

The tall, Gothic windows erected in this 13th century church in South Germany are no longer to be seen there; what remains of the original windows is now in the Hessian Landesmuseum in Darmstadt. These details from a window showing Noah in the Ark, like all the others, were painted on glass by an unknown master who is thought by some scholars to have learned the art in France.

the story of

Text from the King James Bible
Pictures and Text Edited by Barbara Brakeley Miller
Designed and produced by Germano Facetti
Background Information by Jacques Le Goff
and Father Jean Danielou S. J.
TIME-LIFE BOOKS NEW YORK

NOAH

told in photographs by Erich Lessing